PHILIPPIANS

MATURING IN THE CHRISTIAN LIFE

WOODROW KROLL

CROSSWAY BOOKS
WHEATON, ILLINOIS

Philippians: Maturing in the Christian Life

Copyright © 2008 by Back to the Bible

Published by Crossway Books
        a publishing ministry of Good News Publishers
        1300 Crescent Street
        Wheaton, Illinois 60187

Cover photo: iStock

First printing, 2008

Printed in the United States of America

ISBN 13: 978-1-43350-122-7
ISBN 10: 1-43350-122-8

Unless otherwise indicated, all Scripture quotations are taken from *The Holy Bible: English Standard Version.*® Copyright © 2001 by Crossway Bibles, a publishing ministry of Good News Publishers. Used by permission. All rights reserved.

Produced with the assistance of The Livingstone Corporation (www.LivingstoneCorp.com).

Project Staff: Neil Wilson

CH		18	17	16	15	14	13	12	11	10	09	08
15	14	13	12	11	10	9	8	7	6	5	4	3	2	1

Table of Contents

How to Use This Study

The entire text to be studied of the Letter to the Philippians from the English Standard Version is printed before each day's devotional reading so everything you need is in one place. While we recommend reading the Scripture passage before you read the devotional, some have found it helpful to use the devotional as preparation for reading the Scripture. If you are unfamiliar with the English Standard Version (on which this series of studies is based), you might consider reading the included Bible selection, followed by the devotional, and then read the passage again from a different Bible text with which you are more familiar. This will give you an excellent biblical preparation for considering the rest of the lesson.

After each devotional, there are three sections designed to help you better understand and apply the lesson's Scripture passage.

Consider It—Several questions that will give you a better understanding of the Scripture passage. These could also be used for a small group discussion.

Express It—Suggestions for turning the insights from the lesson into prayer.

Go Deeper—Throughout this study, you will benefit from seeing how the letter to the Philippians fits with the rest of the Bible. This additional section will include other passages and insights from Scripture. The Go Deeper section will also allow you to consider some of the implications of the day's passage for the central theme of the study (Maturing in the Christian Life) as well as other key Scripture themes.

The Perfect Church?

Have you noticed that the longer a person is part of a local church the less enthusiastic they are about describing what a great church it is and inviting others to join? Why is that? How did a congregation that we once thought was perfect turn out to be such a disappointment? Whose problem is that?

Philippians 1:1–11

Greeting

1 Paul and Timothy, servants of Christ Jesus,

To all the saints in Christ Jesus who are at Philippi, with the overseers and deacons:

²Grace to you and peace from God our Father and the Lord Jesus Christ.

Thanksgiving and Prayer

³I thank my God in all my remembrance of you, ⁴always in every prayer of mine for you all making my prayer with joy, ⁵because of your partnership in the gospel from the first day until now. ⁶And I am sure of this, that he who began a good work in you will bring it to completion at the day of Jesus Christ. ⁷It is right for me to feel this way about you all, because I hold you in my heart, for you are all partakers with me of grace, both in my imprisonment and in the defense and confirmation of the gospel.

Key Verse

"And I am sure of this, that he who began a good work in you will bring it to completion at the day of Jesus Christ" (Phil. 1:6).

⁸For God is my witness, how I yearn for you all with the affection of Christ Jesus. ⁹And it is my prayer that your love may abound more and more, with knowledge and all discernment, ¹⁰so that you may approve what is excellent, and so be pure and blameless for the day of Christ, ¹¹filled with the fruit of righteousness that comes through Jesus Christ, to the glory and praise of God.

Go Deeper

The word "love" crowds the pages of the Pauline epistles. Use the following to review the central effect of Paul's focus on love. Romans 12:10 tells us, "Love one another with brotherly affection. Outdo one another in showing honor." A chapter later, Paul echoed Jesus' words about the great commandment (Mark 12:28–34) with his own comment, "Love does no wrong to a neighbor; therefore love is the fulfilling of the law" (Rom. 13:10).

Paul wrote the great love chapter (1 Cor. 13) which ends with his declaration

that "the greatest of these is love" (v.13). He was describing the central roles of faith, hope and love while emphasizing the greater importance of love. In eternity, both faith and hope will be remembered as essential parts of our experience while we lived our lives, but love will be ongoing and constant in the presence of Love Himself.

To the Galatians, Paul expressed the unique concept of serving one another in love. (See Gal. 5:13.) The Ephesians got their challenging walking orders from

(continued)

Go Deeper Continued ...

Paul when he wrote, "And walk in love, as Christ loved us and gave himself up for us, a fragrant offering and sacrifice to God" (Eph. 5:2). He reminded the Colossians that part of his deepest hopes for them and their Laodicean brethren involved their experience of love, "that their hearts may be encouraged, being knit together in love, to reach all the riches of full assurance of understanding and the knowledge of God's mystery, which is Christ" (Col. 2:2).

Paul prayed for the Thessalonians that their love would demonstrate its source: "And may the Lord make you increase and abound in love for one another and for all, as we do for you" (1 Thess. 3:12). The apostle asked Titus to respond to those who had demonstrated love for Paul, "Greet those who love us in the faith. Grace be with you all" (Titus 3:15–16). Paul understood that our relationship with God and one another must be surrounded and permeated with love.

Most Christians would like to be a part of a *perfect church.* Unfortunately, since we're not perfect, as soon as we join, any church ceases to be perfect. Actually there is no such thing as a perfect church. Only Jesus as the Head of the Church is perfect. But that doesn't mean we can't find examples of what the church ought to be, model churches that point us toward perfection. In this study we are calling these *grown-up* churches. In the Bible we find a church as close to the perfect church as any that the apostle Paul ever founded—the church at Philippi.

Even though the Philippian church was not perfect, it displayed at least one of the traits that characterize a mature church. A church on the right track is a church that is growing. Now, when we define the perfect church as one that is *growing*, our minds immediately think of numerical growth. We associate growing churches with *growing* attendance, but does that mean that those churches are becoming grown-up churches?

Here in the twenty-first century, we tend to think the *good* churches are the *big* churches. And the not-so-good ones, the less-than-perfect ones, are the ones that aren't big or getting bigger. When we go back to the first century, however, we discover that

"How are you progressing spiritually today? Are you growing up in the Lord, daily growing in your love for others? Are you growing in your knowledge of the Lord Jesus? Growing in your discernment? Growing in your purity? Growing in your blamelessness?"

numerical increase was not the sole or central measurement for a growing church. (See Acts 2:41, 47; 5:14; 6:1, 7.)

The Philippian church, while it grew in numbers, also grew in other ways that are more important than numbers. Paul mentioned the first when he wrote, "And it is my prayer that your love may abound more and more, with knowledge and all discernment" (Phil. 1:9). Growing numbers don't mean much without growing "love." Paul gave *love* a major emphasis in all his letters; and, therefore, we understand that it was a key factor in Paul's thinking about how a church grows up.

If you're attending a church today and you don't see any love there, they're not walking in love; they're not serving one another in love—if that love is absent, if their hearts are not knit together in love—then it's likely that your church is not a grown-up church. A standing-room-only church is not a truly growing church unless love is growing among its members as well. Paul wanted the Philippians to have a fully developed love. If a church is going to be a grown-up church, the cornerstone of that maturity will be its love for one another.

A church that is committed to growing up as well as growing out will increase not only in love but also in "knowledge." That was Paul's second growth criteria in Philippians 1:9, "that your love may abound more and more, with knowledge and all discernment." If love means practicing what we understand about God, then "knowledge" means expanding what we understand about God. Growth in our knowledge of Jesus Christ always comes as a result of consistent exposure to God's Word. Warren Wiersbe claims, "Christian living depends on Christian learning; duty is always founded on doctrine. If Satan can keep a Christian ignorant, he can keep him impotent."*

Further, a grown-up church increases not only in love and knowledge; but also in "discernment," knowing what it ought to love and what it ought to hate. Love without knowledge and discernment is not God's kind of love. God doesn't love blindly. God doesn't love sin. God loves but also corrects, rebukes and even disciplines believers engaged in sin. Paul reminded the Philippians (and us) that growth in real love is characterized by our knowledge of the Word and also characterized by discernment. This is love guided by truth.

But Paul wasn't finished praying for the Philippians to grow up as a church. In the next verse he wrote, "So that you may approve what is excellent, and so be pure and blameless for the day of Christ" (1:10).

The word "approve" means that we grow in our preferences as well. Growing up spiritually involves not only the ability to discern but the actual exercise of that ability: discerning the better and choosing the better every time. The word *pure* means "sincere," a church with no need to make excuses when it stands before Christ. The term is used of precious metals from which all the waste, or impurities, has been extracted. Paul is praying that the Philippians would not exhibit mixed messages to the world but demonstrate "the fruit of righteousness" (v. 11)—grown-up spiritual behavior.

The church in the twenty-first century is in danger of allowing what is good to rob us of what is best. We're attending church and enjoying entertainment and biblical teaching. Those add up to good experiences in church—but not the best experiences. Why? Because

*Warren Wiersbe, *Be Right* (Wheaton, IL: Victor Books, 1977), 61.

that's not growing up. We're not growing the way we need to grow, the way Paul prayed the Philippian church would continue to grow.

How are you progressing spiritually today? Are you growing up in the Lord, *daily* growing in your love for others? Are you growing in your knowledge of the Lord Jesus? Growing in your discernment? Growing in your purity? Growing in your blamelessness? Developing these traits allows you to have a part in making your local church a grown-up church.

Express It

As you pray, consider what the Lord might want to do through you to bring about the traits of a grown-up church in your church. If your church "lacks something," it may be an indication that God wants to supply love, discernment and the fruit of righteousness through you.

Consider It

As you read Philippians 1:1–11, consider these questions:

1) To whom did Paul address this letter? What can we say about this group based on Paul's greeting?

_____

_____

2) What would it mean to you to be offered "grace and peace from God our Father and the Lord Jesus Christ" as a greeting?

_____

_____

3) What does Paul say is the cause of his joy when he prays for the Philippians (vv. 4–5)?

_____

_____

4) How do you apply verse 6 to your own life and relationship with Christ?

_____

_____

5) How did Paul describe his relationship with the Philippians (vv. 7–8)?

_____

_____

6) In what ways would Paul's prayer help you pray more effectively for other Christians?

_____

_____

7) How is "the day of Christ" (v. 10) an accountability point for you?

_____

_____

8) Describe what you consider as some of the "fruit of righteousness" (v. 11).

_____

_____

Grown-up Perspective

Paul was between a Roman rock and a hard place. He was in prison for the Gospel. Death was a definite possibility. Yet he thought of his Philippian friends for comfort and encouragement. What do you do when the way is dark and the day is gloomy?

Philippians 1:12–30

The Advance of the Gospel

[12]I want you to know, brothers, that what has happened to me has really served to advance the gospel, [13]so that it has become known throughout the whole imperial guard and to all the rest that my imprisonment is for Christ. [14]And most of the brothers, having become confident in the Lord by my imprisonment, are much more bold to speak the word without fear.

[15]Some indeed preach Christ from envy and rivalry, but others from good will. [16]The latter do it out of love, knowing that I am put here for the defense of the gospel. [17]The former proclaim Christ out of rivalry, not sincerely but thinking to afflict me in my imprisonment. [18]What then? Only that in every way, whether in pretense or in truth, Christ is proclaimed, and in that I rejoice.

To Live Is Christ

Yes, and I will rejoice, [19]for I know that through your prayers and the help of the Spirit of Jesus Christ this will turn out for my deliverance, [20]as it is my eager expectation and hope that I will not be at all ashamed, but that with full courage now as always Christ will be honored in my body, whether by life or by death.

[21]For to me to live is Christ, and to die is gain. [22]If I am to live in the flesh, that means fruitful labor for me. Yet which I shall choose I cannot tell. [23]I am hard pressed between the two. My desire is to depart and be with Christ, for that is far better. [24]But to remain in the flesh is more necessary on your account. [25]Convinced of this, I know that I will remain and continue with you all, for your progress and joy in the faith, [26]so that in me you may have ample cause to glory in Christ Jesus, because of my coming to you again.

[27]Only let your manner of life be worthy of the gospel of Christ, so that whether I come and see you or am absent, I may hear of you that you are standing firm in one spirit, with one mind striving side by side for the faith of the gospel, [28]and not frightened in anything by your opponents. This is a clear sign to them of their destruction, but of your salvation, and that from God. [29]For it has been granted to you that for the sake of Christ you should not only believe in him but also suffer for his sake, [30]engaged in the same conflict that you saw I had and now hear that I still have.

Key Verse

"For to me to live is Christ, and to die is gain" (Phil. 1:21).

Go Deeper

Paul could have been overwhelmed in prison. News wasn't all that encouraging. "Some indeed preach Christ from envy and rivalry, but others from good will" (v. 15). But for Paul, bad news didn't matter as long as it turned out to be good news for the Gospel of Christ! "What then? Only that in every way, whether in pretense or in truth, Christ is proclaimed, and in that I rejoice. Yes, and I will rejoice" (v. 18). Note here how Paul demonstrates the double "rejoice" that he later commands the Philippians (and us) to practice: "Rejoice in the Lord always; again I will say, Rejoice" (4:4).

Paul knew some people were preaching Christ out of envy and strife. He did not accuse those envious and strife-filled preachers of being false teachers. They were heralding Christ just as Paul was. They were being ambassadors for Christ just as he was. Their message was right, though their motives were wrong.

You will know you are a part of a church that is growing up when, like Paul, in the midst of bad times or criticism or difficult days, you are still committed—your pastor and the people—to magnifying Christ. Paul says, "Look, whatever happens to me, I'm going to magnify Christ. I am committed to helping others see Christ whether my life circumstances are good or not." Paul's life wasn't made up of just bad times, and yours won't be either. The life of your church won't be made up of only bad times; there will be good times too. But good times or bad times—they both mean more when we magnify Christ.

I t's easy to rejoice when things are going well. But joy takes on a different texture when we think about it surrounded by hurt, helplessness and hopelessness. That was Paul's situation when he began his letter to the Philippians. We can't appreciate the joyful tone of this letter unless we picture these words first echoing in the dark hallways of a Roman prison, flowing from the heart of a man who had reached a grown-up perspective on life. When we realize we can't lose what is really most important, we can say with Paul, "For to me to live is Christ, and to die is gain" (1:21).

Deciding to rejoice is not quite the same as deciding to be upbeat. Joy is not optimism. Joy isn't the skill of finding the silver thread in the tangle of life. Joy recognizes that life is an amazing mixture of the wearing and the wonderful. Joy expresses the words of

> **"***As soon as we . . . decide that God has called us to grow up in Christ, we can expect resistance.***"**

Carolina Sandell Berg's well-known hymn, "Day by Day":

> *Day by day, and with each passing moment,*
> *Strength I find to meet my trials here;*
> *Trusting in my Father's wise bestowment,*
> *I've no cause for worry or for fear.*
> *He whose heart is kind beyond all measure,*
> *Gives unto each day what He deems best—*
> *Lovingly, its part of pain and pleasure,*
> *Mingling toil with peace and rest.*

Paul had a grown-up perspective, the ability to rejoice despite circumstances. And he was willing to share that joy with others. He knew the Philippians would understand. They probably remembered with a certain amount of humor that their original encounter with Paul involved a dramatic but brief imprisonment in their local jail. God had shaken open the prison in the middle of the night and set the jailer free! (See Acts 16:16–40.)

A church will not grow up without grown-up leaders. Paul gives us an indelible example of the character of a mature leader. He presented himself to his original readers, as they say, "warts and all." He hid nothing. His self-disclosures don't read like slick public relations pieces, careful to present the best side of the great apostle so others will be impressed. He was a leader with limitations, and he knew them. He was a leader quick to let those following him know that they could imitate him, but only to the degree that he was imitating Christ. (See 1 Cor. 4:16; 11:1.)

So, Paul let the Philippians (and us) in on his thought-life about his circumstances. He didn't sugarcoat the difficulties. He didn't minimize the disappointments. But by revealing the whole picture to his readers, Paul let the Philippians know he trusted them to understand. He knew they would not grow up without knowing what the grown-up life was like—and that it wasn't easy.

In this lesson's passage, verses 27–30 serve as an effective challenge by a mature leader. Paul did not assume he would have ongoing opportunities to impact the Philippians. So, he gave them a glimpse of his expectations. Whether he showed up or not, he wanted them to "let your manner of life be worthy of the gospel of Christ . . . standing firm in one spirit, with one mind striving side by side for the faith of the gospel" (1:27). Paul sketched for the believers in Philippi a verbal picture of a grown-up. The rest of the letter would fill in details, but here at the start Paul wanted his friends to know that he had high expectations for them. He wanted them to face, but not be afraid of, the resistance they would experience in the world. He made it very clear to them what growing up in Christ involved: to "not only believe in him but also suffer for his sake, engaged in the same conflict that you saw I had and now hear that I still have" (1:29–30).

Just as physical growth defies gravity, spiritual growth defies the spiritual gravity of our fallen nature. Growth triggers resistance. As long as we settle for casual, immature faith, life can seem easy and mundane, though pointless. But as soon as we, as individuals or as a church, decide that God has called us to grow up in Christ, we can expect resistance. In fact, if we are not experiencing some kind of resistance, we can be quite certain we are not growing up spiritually. Paul's conclusion needs to become our daily prayer: "For to me to live is Christ, and to die is gain." Living by those words is evidence of genuine spiritual growth and a grown-up perspective.

Express It

Before you pray, write down a list of at least ten circumstances in your life right now that may be difficult but for which you are willing to rejoice because of what God can do in and through you in those situations. Then, as you pray, work through the list and practice rejoicing!

Consider It

As you read Philippians 1:12–30, consider these questions:

1) What hardships was Paul experiencing in prison?

_____

_____

2) How did he turn some of the bad news of people's responses to his imprisonment into good news? (See vv. 15–18.)

_____

_____

3) Even in jail, Paul found a special audience. Who were they?

_____

_____

4) How well have you learned to identify both the blows and the benefits of difficult situations in your life? What difference does this skill make?

_____

_____

5) In what ways does Paul report joy throughout this passage?

_____

_____

6) What kind of progress does Paul refer to in verse 25? How does it echo the theme of this study?

_____

_____

7) What persons in your life have demonstrated a grown-up perspective to you? How?

_____

_____

8) In what areas of your life are you experiencing the resistance that indicates spiritual growth?

_____

_____

The Ultimate Pattern

Most of us realize it's hard to grow up without good role models. Physical growth may be somewhat inevitable, but growth in other ways depends on support, direction and help. If we want to grow spiritually in a healthy way, we will also need a good model. Jesus gives us that.

Philippians 2:1–11

Christ's Example of Humility

2 So if there is any encouragement in Christ, any comfort from love, any participation in the Spirit, any affection and sympathy, ²complete my joy by being of the same mind, having the same love, being in full accord and of one mind. ³Do nothing from rivalry or conceit, but in humility count others more significant than yourselves. ⁴Let each of you look not only to his own interests, but also to the interests of others. ⁵Have this mind among yourselves, which is yours in Christ Jesus, ⁶who, though he was in the form of God, did not count equality with God a thing to be grasped, ⁷but made himself nothing, taking the form of a servant, being born in the likeness of men. ⁸And being found in human form, he humbled himself by becoming obedient to the point of death, even death on a cross. ⁹Therefore God has highly exalted him and bestowed on him the name that is above every name, ¹⁰so that at the name of Jesus every knee should bow, in heaven and on earth and under the earth, ¹¹and every tongue confess that Jesus Christ is Lord, to the glory of God the Father.

Key Verse

"Have this mind among yourselves, which is yours in Christ Jesus"(Phil. 2:5).

Go Deeper

In the notes later on we touch on the importance of the mind in Paul's letter to the Philippians. Central to that theme is the mind of Christ, described in this lesson's passage. The mind of Christ led to the radical change in Christ's status as God with relation to the world. That change can be summarized in three phases, best viewed in descending order. We begin with His eternal position—in the form of God (v. 6). Second, He took on the form of a servant (literally, a "slave") (v. 7). Third, in order to carry out His assignment, He assumed every aspect of His servant role up to and including death on a cross (v. 8).

In the mind of Christ, nothing got between Him and the mission He had accepted to be the Servant-Savior, the Suffering-Savior, the Solitary-Savior.

On the cross Jesus submitted to the lowest form of death. His declension (lowering/emptying) was complete. Jesus gave up the riches of glory for our sakes (2 Cor. 8:9; John 17:5). Without every phase of His emptying, we could not have atonement for our sin (Heb. 2:17–18). Our best response is to pattern His mind and exalt His person with all we've got!

For followers of Jesus, growing up is growing to be *like* Christ. The more we grow into Christ-likeness, the more we will be grown up in every way. We might say that Jesus is the ultimate grown-up, and all of us want to be like Him. Our best desires and the qualities we long to have reflect His perfect character whether we realize it.

Paul related his thanks for the Philippians and assured them of his prayers in the first chapter of his letter; now he points them directly to Christ. He lets them know that their ultimate motivation shouldn't be to please him but to please and imitate Christ. Others may even "proclaim Christ out of rivalry" (1:17), but Paul expects the Philippians to "do nothing from rivalry or conceit, but in humility count others more significant than yourselves" (2:3).

Some Bible translations don't make it obvious, but Paul clearly had the mind of Christians in his thoughts when he wrote this letter. The word *mind* that appears twice in verse 2, along with the "mind" found in the key verse (v. 5), literally means "thinking." That's why it is often translated "attitude." The way we think and the things that really occupy our minds eventually become clear through our actions. Early in the letter, when he described his prayer for the Philippians, much of the apostle's desire for these believers involved the state of their minds, asking God not only to increase their love but to add knowledge and discernment to it—traits that involve grown-up minds. At the end of the first chapter, Paul told his friends that he longed to hear "that you are standing firm in one spirit, *with one mind* striving side by side for the faith of the gospel" (1:27, italics added). But here the word "mind" is literally *soul,* indicating a centrality of purpose. Later, in 3:15–19, Paul includes another section on the central effects of what occupies our minds.

The connection between love and a grown-up mind is an often overlooked biblical theme. Because we tend to equate love with feelings, we forget that genuine love is as much about the mind as it is about the heart. Authentic, grown-up love is not just heartfelt but thoughtful. Jesus made this connection when He quoted the Great Commandment: "And you shall love the Lord your God with all your heart and with all your soul and with all your mind and with all your

"Saying "Jesus is Lord" ... [is about being] perfectly comfortable with His Lordship, no matter what happens to us."

strength" (Mark 12:30). When Paul expounded on the amazing complexities of the kind of love that God wants to pour into our lives (1 Cor. 13), he added an important reminder that the kind of love he was describing was a God-sourced, grown-up kind of love exercised with an adult mind: "When I was a child, I spoke like a child, I thought like a child, I reasoned like a child. When I became a man, I gave up childish ways" (1 Cor. 13:11). Paul had grown up in Christ, and he wanted others to experience that same maturity.

So, Paul pointed them (and us) directly to the Lord: "Have this mind among yourselves, which is yours in Christ Jesus" (Phil. 2:5). It's worth noting that the phrase "among yourselves" has often and can be translated "in you" (plural you), giving it a dual sense that the Philippians needed to develop personal as well as corporate attitudes that reflected Christ's character. There's an uncanny sense in which churches develop "minds"—a corporate personality and attitude. These deeply ingrained ways of thinking can affect everyone and be difficult to identify from the inside. But they are often obvious to outsiders. An unwelcome, lethargic or judgmental church may be quite satisfied with their condition, but those who visit are repelled by the lack of Christ-likeness.

What does it mean for a Christian or a group of Christians to have Christ's mind? In a word, Christ showed us *humility*. He had the right to remain God, but He chose to take on humanity. We have a subtle (and sometimes obvious) tendency to want to claim godhood, and humility is a very difficult trait for many of us to exercise. It's the opposite of pride, which is at the center of our human rebellion against God. Jesus gave up His rightful place for our benefit. Humility for us begins in seeing Jesus clearly in His rightful place and treating Him that way. Personal obedience, corporate worship and relationships all exhibit humility when Jesus is really at the center. The point of saying "Jesus is Lord" isn't about mouthing the right words; it's about living in a way that shows others we know what Jesus' title means; and we are perfectly comfortable with His Lordship, no matter what happens to us.

Humility leaves any kind of acclaim up to God. Jesus did not exalt Himself. Philippians 2:8–9 tells us that God the Father responded to Jesus' humility by restoring Him to His rightful place when His work was finished. Until we resist temptations to exalt ourselves, we haven't developed the grown-up mindset that can practice humility.

Express It

As you pray, spend a few moments thinking about the way you visualize Jesus. How do you picture Him in your mind—not what He looks like, but who He is? Does your mental image lead you to worship Him? Is that image just another picture in your mental album, or does the very thought of Christ fill you with a sense of awe and a desire to bow in humble adoration? How often do you ask Him for His mind?

Consider It

As you read Philippians 2:1–11, consider these questions:

1) How many "ifs" does Paul use on which to base his call to single-mindedness in Christ? (See 2:1 in the NKJV or NASB versions. Some of these are implied in the ESV but not stated.)

_____

_____

_____

2) What three developments among the Philippians does Paul say will "complete" his joy?

_____

_____

_____

3) What experiences of one-mindedness in Christ have you participated in during your life?

_____

_____

_____

4) How do we get the mind of Christ?

_____

_____

_____

5) What four actions did Jesus take in practicing humility?

_____

_____

_____

6) How will God exalt Jesus at the end of time?

_____

_____

_____

7) If God promises that "every knee should bow" and "every tongue confess that Jesus Christ is Lord," (vv. 10–11) how should we respond now?

_____

_____

_____

A Grown-up Purpose

Some people spend years hopping from church to church looking for perfection. That's a pointless search. What should we look for in a local church? Is the church a place where we serve or a place that serves us? Paul knew the difference, and he saw it in Philippi.

Philippians 2:12–18

Lights in the World

¹²Therefore, my beloved, as you have always obeyed, so now, not only as in my presence but much more in my absence, work out your own salvation with fear and trembling, ¹³for it is God who works in you, both to will and to work for his good pleasure.

¹⁴Do all things without grumbling or questioning, ¹⁵that you may be blameless and innocent, children of God without blemish in the midst of a crooked and twisted generation, among whom you shine as lights in the world, ¹⁶holding fast to the word of life, so that in the day of Christ I may be proud that I did not run in vain or labor in vain. ¹⁷Even if I am to be poured out as a drink offering upon the sacrificial offering of your faith, I am glad and rejoice with you all. ¹⁸Likewise you also should be glad and rejoice with me.

Key Verse

"For it is God who works in you, both to will and to work for his good pleasure" (Phil. 2:13).

Go Deeper

Grown-ups and grown-up churches are not immune to problems. There's always room to grow, and sometimes we have to grow again in ways we have already grown. Paul touched on the issues of "grumbling" and "questioning" in Philippians 2:14. These two problems can almost instantly derail a group making good progress and shatter peace.

God has a long-standing policy regarding grumbling, demonstrated in detail in the Old Testament. That attitude was among several that God confronted when He doomed a generation of Israelites to die in the wilderness. Elsewhere (1 Cor. 10:1–5, 10) the New Testament uses this painful episode in Israel's history to warn about the habit of grumbling.

The word *questioning* means "to debate." Many versions translate it "disputing." Disputing is usually a symptom of pride in action.

Paul dealt with this at length in 1 Corinthians 6:1–11. The alternate attitudes Paul described for the Philippians help us see why grumbling and questioning are destructive. First, they weaken and disrupt unity. The singleness of mind Paul urges can't be maintained with these attitudes (Phil. 2:2). Second, grumbling and questioning have no place in those demonstrating Christ's attitude of humility (vv. 5–8). Third, the watching world will not be drawn to Christ if those who claim to know Him can't get along (v. 15).

Not only does a mature church have a growing component to it, a grown-up church also has a commitment to missions. You usually can tell the health of a church by its attitude toward missions. But remember, missions is not just "out there" somewhere; missions is also "near here." It's to the ends of the earth beginning with our next-door neighbor. God's good pleasure is to drive us to be channels of the Gospel to the world.

When Andrew began to follow the Lord Jesus, the first thing he did was find his own brother, Peter, and tell him he'd found the Messiah. When Philip began to follow the Lord Jesus, the first thing he did was find his friend Nathanael. That's not exactly foreign missions, is it? After Isaiah made that great speech to the Lord God, "Here am I, Lord; send me," God said, "Okay, Isaiah, go back to your own people and give them My Word." (See Isa. 6.)

There are always challenges that come up when we talk about the relationship between the local church and missions, particularly the relationship of the church to those doing mission work. Paul's relationship with the Philippians gives us some insights into the important two-way personal connections between the local church and the work of missions. The point of clarification, Paul tells us in Philippians 2:15–16, is to make sure that we all "shine as lights in the world, holding fast to the word of life."

Paul wrote this letter, in part, to address questions that had risen about his character. His connection with the Philippians was in danger. Some of the events in Paul's life that probably precipitated his writing could be interpreted several ways. For example, Paul went to Thessalonica after he was at Philippi (Acts 17:1), and there he was persecuted by the religious Jews of that city. Multitudes believed in the Gospel, and Paul was accused of turning the world upside down. (Actually, he turned the world right side up). But this also gave him, in some quarters, a reputation as a troublemaker. He was forced to flee from the city under the cover of darkness. Meanwhile, believers in Philippi were supporting Paul financially (Phil. 4:15–16).

Eventually, mixed messages came back to Philippi. Paul's reputation was under attack. Imagine the rumors and innuendos, the

"How aware are you of the struggles and successes being experienced by those who represent your church in the work of missions?"

questions about his use of funds from believers, about his hasty departure during the middle of the night. These reports easily could have destroyed the church's trust in their "missionary." In fact, they probably would have if it were not for one thing—the character of Paul.

What would cause a local church not to have a trusting relationship with those representing their passion for missions? What could cause folks in mission work to wonder about those "at home"? Distance for one thing and lack of communication for another. Mission support is much more than finances. It's also informed prayer. When Paul wrote to the churches who were supporting him as well as to those he wanted to help, he always assured them of his prayers. His prayers demonstrate that he understood what they needed (Phil. 1:3–11)! And he made sure through his letters that they knew what he needed (Phil. 4:10–20). The trust went two ways. Paul kept the lines of communication open.

When we as a church are developing our missions commitments, we must choose them carefully; we must trust those we have chosen to represent us explicitly. Diligence should be exercised in the choosing! If you want to be a part of a missionary church, a church that is as grown up as it can be, make sure that your church has a two-way trusting relationship with those involved in missions. Modern technology may make this easier today than in Paul's day, but we still need to communicate.

But trust is not the only thing we learn about the Philippians and Paul. The apostle also says, "Even if I am to be poured out as a drink offering upon the sacrificial offering of your faith, I am glad and rejoice with you all. Likewise you also should be glad and rejoice with me" (Phil. 2:17–18).

We need a two-way trusting relationship with our missionaries, but we also need a two-way rejoicing relationship. Any church that wants to be as near perfect as it can be needs to have an encouraging/rejoicing relationship with those involved in all facets of missions. We have to keep our friendships in constant repair, especially our friendships with those who represent our mission commitment at home and abroad. In order "to weep with those who weep and rejoice with those who rejoice" (see Rom. 12:15), we first need to communicate! How aware are you of the struggles and successes being experienced by those who represent your church in the work of missions?

Again, the point of all this is the effect of the church in the world. The impact of the Gospel on us is measured by the degree to which we feel compelled to pass it on to others. The idea behind "work out your own salvation" (2:12) has nothing to do with earning salvation but rather refers to living out what God has worked in us. That's why Paul immediately reminded his friends that God is behind both our desires and our efforts to spread the Good News. Paul always made sure he communicated confidence and gladness in his two-way relationships with "growing-up" churches.

Express It

When we pray for our church, we must consider what God might want to tell us about our role in helping this body of believers develop the attitude of Christ. We don't pray in isolation; we pray as participants. How are you, as a member of the Body, praying for the Body of Christ?

Consider It

As you read Philippias 2:12–18, consider these questions:

1) How does Paul review his past relationship with the Philippians as a basis for his next commands?

_____

_____

2) In what ways has God promised to participate in our spiritual growth (v. 13)?

_____

_____

3) What, in these verses, indicates the traits that make it difficult for Christians to "shine as lights in the world"?

_____

_____

4) How does Paul describe the condition of the world surrounding the Philippian church?

_____

_____

5) What two pictures does Paul use to describe his work among the Philippian believers (v. 16)?

_____

_____

6) How far was Paul willing to go in securing the faith of the Philippians (v. 17)? Why?

_____

_____

7) Have you ever received an uplifting note that encouraged you to be a "light in the world," written by someone deeply influential in your life? What does Paul's note mean to you?

_____

_____

Outside Help

Paul was always a team player. He traveled with others making the most of combined efforts. As an apostle, he continuously built into others, preparing them to take over the work. He practiced what he preached.

Philippians 2:19–30

Timothy and Epaphroditus

¹⁹I hope in the Lord Jesus to send Timothy to you soon, so that I too may be cheered by news of you. ²⁰For I have no one like him, who will be genuinely concerned for your welfare. ²¹For they all seek their own interests, not those of Jesus Christ. ²²But you know Timothy's proven worth, how as a son with a father he has served with me in the gospel. ²³I hope therefore to send him just as soon as I see how it will go with me, ²⁴and I trust in the Lord that shortly I myself will come also.

²⁵I have thought it necessary to send to you Epaphroditus my brother and fellow worker and fellow soldier, and your messenger and minister to my need, ²⁶for he has been longing for you all and has been distressed because you heard that he was ill. ²⁷Indeed he was ill, near to death. But God had mercy on him, and not only on him but on me also, lest I should have sorrow upon sorrow. ²⁸I am the more eager to send him, therefore, that you may rejoice at seeing him again, and that I may be less anxious. ²⁹So receive him in the Lord with all joy, and honor such men, ³⁰for he nearly died for the work of Christ, risking his life to complete what was lacking in your service to me.

> ## Key Verse
>
> *"But you know Timothy's proven worth, how as a son with a father he has served with me in the gospel"* (Phil. 2:22).

Go Deeper

Epaphroditus is only mentioned in the Bible in the book of Philippians (Phil. 2:25; 4:18). The fact that we have the letter to the Philippians in our New Testaments tells us that Epaphroditus completed not only the task given to him by his church in Philippi but also the task Paul entrusted to him of carrying this Spirit-inspired letter back to his hometown.

Paul and others were aware, even when the letters were still in their original form, that his writings conveyed what God wanted written—that they were God's Word. (See 2 Pet. 3:15–16.) Imagine Epaphroditus's journey of a thousand miles by foot and sea to carry Paul's precious letter to Philippi. We owe him thanks.

We know considerably more about Timothy. Not only did he travel extensively with and for the apostle Paul, he also received at least two letters from the apostle that make up two-thirds of what are traditionally known as Paul's Pastoral Epistles (1 and 2 Timothy and Titus). Paul's letters make it clear that he considered Timothy the person he most trusted to carry on his ministry. Many people served on Paul's team; some of them disappointed him but not Timothy. He was his trusted son in the faith.

The first time the Philippians met Paul, they also met Timothy and Silas. (See Acts 16.) Silas was a leader in the Jerusalem church and a veteran traveler with Paul. But Timothy had recently joined Paul's team and was rapidly gaining experience "on the road" as Paul spread the Gospel. At their first official mission stop, Philippi, imagine how Timothy felt when both his mentors were thrown in prison and he was the only team member still free. Fortunately, the midnight upheaval at the prison put the team back together again. But the experience of that crisis appears to have formed a special bond between the believers in Philippi and Timothy. When Paul wrote to the Philippians later, he pointedly named the writers of the letter as "Paul and Timothy, servants of Christ Jesus" (Phil. 1:1). In this lesson's passage, Paul promised to send Timothy to the church again.

Paul also mentioned Epaphroditus, who had come to Rome from Philippi, bringing messages and support from the church. On the journey or when he arrived in Rome, Epaphroditus became ill and nearly died. The news of his condition had reached Philippi, and Epaphroditus knew the church there was concerned about him. Now he would be returning with Paul's letter.

Paul took time in this letter to offer commendations about two of his teammates. He compared his relationship with Timothy to the best a father and son can have. The people of Philippi were witnesses to the early days of that relationship, and they would benefit from the grown-up leader that Timothy was becoming. He used the term "proven worth" (2:22) to describe one of the components of spiritual maturity. Paul's relationship with Timothy was far more than traveling companions. Timothy had been a participant in the ups and downs of ministry with Paul. He had endured. He wasn't just an interested observer; he had been involved. Paul saw his proven role as a fellow servant—they had been places, seen things and accomplished much for God. Timothy had demonstrated in the heat of battle that Paul could count on him. That's why Paul could confidently tell the Philippians they also could count on Timothy. As a "son," Timothy could faithfully represent his father in the faith, Paul. Apart from coming himself, which Paul clearly longed to do, he could think of no one better to send than Timothy.

" Those who are grown up in Christ make it their overriding priority to find ways to serve others. But they also learn that being part of the Body of Christ means accepting the special services that God has designed for others to exercise in ministry. "

The warm remarks Paul wrote about Epaphroditus are a classic example of how to highlight another person's abilities and effectiveness. The apostle gave him five titles: brother, fellow worker, fellow soldier, your messenger and your minister to my need (v. 25). These must have had a powerful effect on the Philippians' view of their emissary. Whatever the reasons for choosing to send Epaphroditus, their choice was certainly confirmed and affirmed by Paul. But these words of affirmation must have had an immeasurable effect on Epaphroditus. In "brother," Paul affirmed Epaphroditus's shared relationship with Christ, the deepest connection between believers. With "fellow worker," Paul expressed appreciation for Epaphroditus's effectiveness in the work of spreading the Gospel. By adding "fellow soldier," Paul saluted Epaphroditus's commitment to the task, his willingness to face dangers out of obedience to Christ. In the term "your messenger" we find Paul's affirmation of Epaphroditus's effective service on behalf of the believers in Philippi, carrying out the task of expressing their support and delivering their gifts. Even more than that, in the term "minister" Paul was letting the Philippians know that in Epaphroditus's efforts and care Paul had experienced directly what the Philippians would have all liked to have done for Paul.

Jesus' instruction to His followers in Matthew 20:26–28 included a delightful but challenging step. He made it one of the central hallmarks of the believers. He said, "Whoever would be great among you must be your servant, and whoever would be first among you must be your slave, even as the Son of Man came not to be served but to serve, and to give his life as a ransom for many" (Matt. 20:26–28). Paul certainly knew what it meant to serve, but he also understood how to graciously accept service and help from others. The priority for followers of Jesus is service. Those who are grown up in Christ make it their overriding priority to find ways to serve others. But they also learn that being part of the Body of Christ means accepting the special services that God has designed for others to exercise in ministry. No servant is an independent or self-sufficient operator. Each of us who is serving Christ and others will find that He provides people like Timothy and Epaphroditus along the way who do for us what we cannot do for ourselves—and do with us what we could not do alone.

Express It

Before praying, consider the people who have served as "Pauls" in your life. Think about the people who have been most like Timothy and Epaphroditus for you. Then begin to tell God how you appreciate the gifts these people have delivered into your life. Ask Him for wisdom in doing your part to serve even those who have served you.

Consider It

As you read Philippians 2:19–30, consider these questions:

1) What did Paul say was his purpose in planning to send Timothy to Philippi?

_____

_____

_____

2) When was Paul planning to send Timothy? Why?

_____

_____

_____

3) In what way did Paul and Timothy's relationship parallel the kind of relationship you want to have with your spiritual mentors?

_____

_____

_____

4) Which of Paul's descriptive terms for Epaphroditus would you most like to have used in describing you? In what ways?

_____

_____

_____

5) What do you think Paul appreciated most about having Timothy and Epaphroditus with him in Rome?

_____

_____

_____

6) In looking at Timothy and Epaphroditus (see Going Deeper), with which one of these believers do you most closely identify? Why?

_____

_____

_____

7) What traits do other Christians notice most in you?

_____

_____

_____

The Grown-up Life

All of us, consciously or not, are trying to live a life that makes sense. An aimless, purposeless, meaningless life attracts few fans. Those who conclude that their lives are little more than that often despair and even end their lives. What brings central meaning to life?

Philippians 3:1–11

Righteousness Through Faith in Christ

3 Finally, my brothers, rejoice in the Lord. To write the same things to you is no trouble to me and is safe for you.

[2]Look out for the dogs, look out for the evildoers, look out for those who mutilate the flesh. [3]For we are the circumcision, who worship by the Spirit of God and glory in Christ Jesus and put no confidence in the flesh—[4]though I myself have reason for confidence in the flesh also. If anyone else thinks he has reason for confidence in the flesh, I have more: [5]circumcised on the eighth day, of the people of Israel, of the tribe of Benjamin, a Hebrew of Hebrews; as to the law, a Pharisee; [6]as to zeal, a persecutor of the church; as to righteousness under the law, blameless. [7]But whatever gain I had, I counted as loss for the sake of Christ. [8]Indeed, I count everything as loss because of the surpassing worth of knowing Christ Jesus my Lord. For his sake I have suffered the loss of all things and count them as rubbish, in order that I may gain Christ [9]and be found in him, not having a righteousness of my own that comes from the law, but that which comes through faith in Christ, the righteousness from God that depends on faith—[10]that I may know him and the power of his resurrection, and may share his sufferings, becoming like him in his death, [11]that by any means possible I may attain the resurrection from the dead.

Key Verse

"Indeed, I count everything as loss because of the surpassing worth of knowing Christ Jesus my Lord. For his sake I have suffered the loss of all things and count them as rubbish, in order that I may gain Christ" (Phil. 3:8).

Go Deeper

How easy is it for you to say, "I know Jesus Christ"? How would you describe what it means to you to know Christ? Twice in this lesson's passage, Paul uses this expression (vv. 8, 10) to refer to his relationship with Jesus. In the English language the word *know* conveys very different meanings. When we say we know someone and when we say we know how to solve a math problem, we are talking about two kinds of knowledge: relational knowing and factual knowing. Relational knowing is open-ended. When we know someone, there's always more to know. Factual knowing has boundaries. We can get close to knowing everything about a certain subject or skill.

Knowing Christ Jesus our Lord is the greatest relational connection a human being can have. Intimacy with God is a humbling, saving and challenging possibility for the Christian. As Paul declared, nothing compares with it. It is experiencing now, with some limits, what we will experience—without boundaries—in eternity. Jesus said, "And this is eternal life, that they *know* you the only true God, and Jesus Christ whom you have sent" (John 17:3, italics added). Can you say you know Jesus Christ? If not, He certainly wants to know you!

Christ's towering example as well as Timothy and Epaphroditus's peer examples filled the second chapter of Philippians. Now, Paul returns to a heartfelt warning about the pressure he knew the Philippians were under to veer away from the grown-up life of joy and freedom in Christ and back into the captivity of erroneous teachings about human effort and "confidence in the flesh" (v. 3). He already mentioned he knew they were facing "opponents" (1:28), but he didn't want them to be afraid of their enemies' authority or persuasiveness. As long as the Philippians were "standing firm in one spirit, with one mind striving side by side for the faith of the gospel" (1:27), they would have nothing to worry about.

Paul realized that teachers with impressive credentials would show up in Philippi and contradict the Gospel of faith in Christ. They would challenge Paul's authority and insist that followers of Jesus must submit to the practices of Judaism before they could be right with God. At the top of the list was the demand that Gentiles be circumcised as a requirement for acceptance. Paul used very strong language to reject this alternative to the Gospel. He acknowledged that circumcision had a role in Jewish culture (See Rom. 4.), but he rejected the idea that God required all people to be circumcised. What God does require of all is repentance and faith in Christ. Paul didn't use the usual term in referring to circumcision but called it "mutilating the flesh." (See v. 2.) His point was that "confidence in the flesh" is based on what is done *in* the flesh and *to* the flesh, but the flesh (human efforts and achievements) cannot win favor with God. "If it could, Paul declares, I would be at the head of the line." (See vv. 4–5.)

The apostle next describes his Jewish pedigree (vv. 5–6). His list was impressive. He surpassed the standard criteria for "righteousness under the law, blameless" (v. 6). Not only had he lived the life, he had enthusiastically persecuted those who dared to follow Jesus Christ. Paul knew he could "out-Judaize the Judaizers," but he also knew from experience that success in does religious life does not add up to spiritual freedom or peace with God. He understood that right standing with God never comes out of our efforts *for* God but out of what God does *in* us. Until we are surrendered to God, even our best efforts act as barriers between God and us. We are still exercising confidence in

> ❝*Right standing with God never comes out of our efforts for God but out of what God does in us.*❞

the flesh, trying to gain or earn something from God that He wants to give us freely. As long as we insist on earning it or deserving it, we can't receive it. Paul gladly tossed all his credentials aside because he knew that much of what impresses other people has little impact on God. He could declare, "But whatever gain I had, I counted as loss for the sake of Christ" (v. 7).

Now, Paul was on a roll. We can imagine his voice thundering through the prison hallways, pushing back the darkness with words of light and hope. "Indeed, I count everything as loss because of the surpassing worth of knowing Christ Jesus my Lord. For his sake I have suffered the loss of all things and count them as rubbish, in order that I may gain Christ" (v. 8)! What was he saying? Was he rejecting his heritage? Didn't he think that his upbringing or his religious training was of any value? Was he turning his back on his own identity? Of course not! He was simply making the deepest value judgment a person can make: Does anything or everything else in my life have ultimate value *when compared with Christ?* It's evident that Paul practiced what Jesus put in very personal terms: "Whoever loves father or mother more than me is not worthy of me, and whoever loves son or daughter more than me is not worthy of me. And whoever does not take his cross and follow me is not worthy of me. Whoever finds his life will lose it, and whoever loses his life for my sake will find it" (Matt. 10:37–39).

Paul used several terms to describe the connection between himself and Christ. The first is "knowing" (vv. 8, 10—see Go Deeper). The second is "gain" Christ (v. 8). As long as we have values that compete with Christ, we don't have room for all that Christ wants to be and can be in our lives. The more we *lose* the things of the world, the more we can *gain* Christ. The third term is "found in him" (v. 9), a delightful expression that pictures a person's location with Christ. It's as if Paul was saying, "I want to live in such a way that if you are looking for me, look for Christ, because that's where I'll be." The New Testament uses both the idea that Christ is in us (Col. 1:27) and that we are in Christ (2 Cor. 5:17) as two sides of the same coin when it comes to our relationship with Him. This is a beautiful expression of the grown-up Christian life: Christ in us and us in Christ.

Express It

Before you pray, read Go Deeper. Think for a few minutes about what it means to know Christ. Consider what might be competing for your attention in the inner areas of your life. Ask God to help you see the things you must consider loss in order to gain Christ and be found in Him. And if you can't honestly say you know Christ, make this the day in which you invite Him to move in and make Himself at home in your life.

Consider It

As you read Philippians 3:1–11, consider these questions:

1) How does Paul describe those who are trying to undermine the faith of the Philippians?

_____

_____

2) What other "confidences in the flesh" do people substitute for faith in Christ?

_____

_____

3) What specific items does Paul list on his religious résumé?

_____

_____

4) How can something have value yet not matter when it comes to the issue of salvation?

_____

_____

5) What things could you list as "gains in life" that you count as loss for the sake of Christ?

_____

_____

6) What happens when we consider everything as nothing compared to Christ, and God takes some of it?

_____

_____

7) How does Paul make a relationship with Christ both challenging and deeply appealing?

_____

_____

8) What part(s) of Paul's relationship with Christ do you long to experience more deeply in your own relationship with Him?

_____

_____

The Upward Pressure

What does it mean to be the kind of person who is constantly progressing onward and upward? Constantly living more like the Master would have you live? Where do you start?

Philippians 3:12–21

Straining Toward the Goal

¹²Not that I have already obtained this or am already perfect, but I press on to make it my own, because Christ Jesus has made me his own. ¹³Brothers, I do not consider that I have made it my own. But one thing I do: forgetting what lies behind and straining forward to what lies ahead, ¹⁴I press on toward the goal for the prize of the upward call of God in Christ Jesus. ¹⁵Let those of us who are mature think this way, and if in anything you think otherwise, God will reveal that also to you. ¹⁶Only let us hold true to what we have attained.

¹⁷Brothers, join in imitating me, and keep your eyes on those who walk according to the example you have in us. ¹⁸For many, of whom I have often told you and now tell you even with tears, walk as enemies of the cross of Christ. ¹⁹Their end is destruction, their god is their belly, and they glory in their shame, with minds set on earthly things. ²⁰But our citizenship is in heaven, and from it we await a Savior, the Lord Jesus Christ, ²¹who will transform our lowly body to be like his glorious body, by the power that enables him even to subject all things to himself.

Key Verse

"But one thing I do: forgetting what lies behind and straining forward to what lies ahead, I press on toward the goal for the prize of the upward call of God in Christ Jesus" (Phil. 3:13–14).

Go Deeper

Paul had a "one thing" (v. 13) outlook on spiritual growth, a process he called "walking" (v. 17). But just as walking involves separate motions, spiritual progress includes, as Paul puts it here, "forgetting," "straining forward" and "pressing on" (vv. 13–14.)

Read the four Prison Epistles and you'll find Paul consistently saying, "You need to plan for me to come," especially to the Philippians, "because I plan to come to you before winter." Even though he was in *prison,* he was looking forward. This is at least part of what it means to "strain forward." It's leaning into life, expecting God to lead and provide. By forgetting the past we don't worry about what's behind, and by straining forward we don't worry about what's ahead. Most of the future we don't know, but Someone does and we can trust Him. And that's the reason we can "press on." That's how we overcome. When Jesus left His memos to the various churches in Revelation 2 and 3, His recurring challenge was to "the one who conquers" (Rev. 2:7, 11, 17, 26; 3:5, 12, 21). When we practice "forgetting," "straining forward" and "pressing on," God ensures we overcome—and grow up along the way.

What is this "upward call" that Paul mentions? He challenges us to the "upward" calling of God, the *heavenward* calling of God. As Christians, we are being drawn like a magnet to true north. We are being drawn heavenward, and every day we should walk on a level a little higher than we walked the day before. We are getting to be more and more like our Savior every day. As He knocks off the rough edges of our lives, and as we understand what His goals are for us, we live in a heavenward manner. Now, what are the essentials of living like that? In terms of these verses, they are "forgetting," "straining forward" and "pressing on." Paul thought of these as one thing. And it's obvious from these words that, for the Christian, growing up is not automatic.

Growing up has a lot to do with forgetting. The Bible has a lot to say about forgetting and about remembering. Here are some examples of the importance of remembering: God put a rainbow in the sky to remember His covenant with Noah never to destroy the earth again with a great flood (Genesis 9:16). The fourth commandment (Ex. 20:8) instructed Israel to remember the Sabbath day and to keep it holy. In Job 10:9, Job asked God to remember his body—that it was like molded clay. Psalm 103:2 tells us, "Bless the Lord, O my soul, and forget not all his benefits." Often, it's good for us to remember.

The Bible also tells us sometimes it's important to forget. In Psalm 25, David prays, "Remember not the sins of my youth or my transgressions; according to your steadfast love remember me, for the sake of your goodness, O Lord!" (Ps. 25:7). There are certain things we don't want God to remember about the way we were when we were teenagers! Isaiah prayed to the Lord God, "Be not so terribly angry, O Lord, and remember not iniquity forever. Behold, please look, we are all your people" (Isa. 64:9). The Bible tells us that it can be good to forget and also good to remember.

According to this lesson's passage, living spiritually grown-up requires us to forget. The phrase "forgetting what lies behind" actually translates a single Greek word. The word *epilanthanomai* simply means "to neglect," "not to care for anymore." The way we forget involves simply neglecting what is behind us. We can forget much of our past if we simply don't keep bringing it up.

❝*One of the greatest mistakes Christians make is forgetting what we should remember and remembering what we should forget. This is sure to invite defeat.***❞**

Unfortunately, we also can forget God's Word if we neglect it. That's not desirable. But "deliberate neglect" is what the word "forget" means. It means not to care about something anymore. The real skill is in knowing what we should remember and knowing what we should forget and not confusing the two. So, when Paul summarized the steps he took to keep growing up in the faith, he started with "forgetting what lies behind."

Paul's life reveals he practiced at least four kinds of forgetting. First, Paul forgot his past failures. He mentioned them when telling the story of God's grace in his life (see his testimony before Agrippa in Acts 26:2–18), but he didn't let them cripple his present life. He didn't see failure as defeat but as a way not to do something again. That's really what failure is—a process of learning and eliminating. We need to learn from our mistakes. He would say to us, "Forget doing those things that you have tried and have not been successful at." We learn from failures; we don't dwell on or in them.

Secondly, the apostle Paul forgot all of his lost opportunities. We need to forget those because we can never recover lost opportunities. We can never go back and have them again. Looking at lost opportunities often prohibits us from seeing present ones. Paul was in prison in Rome. If he were looking at all his lost opportunities there, he would not have seen the present opportunities to witness to the prison guards.

Thirdly, Paul forgot all his successes. He didn't dwell on his achievements. He listed them back in Philippians 3:4–8, but only to report that he considered them a loss in comparison to "the surpassing worth of knowing Christ Jesus my Lord" (v. 8). Nothing can destroy the future faster than success in the past. We need to rejoice in those successes and see their source in God. We need to relish them, but we need to learn humility from them because the same God that gives grace to succeed also gives grace to fail.

Fourth, Paul forgot all of his near successes. When he had to leave town before the work was done, as he did in Philippi (see Acts 16:35–40), he left it in God's hands. Nothing in life robs us of future planning more than going back and remembering near successes and trying to repair them.

One of the greatest mistakes Christians make is forgetting what we should remember and remembering what we should forget. This is sure to invite defeat. "Forgetting those things that are past, straining forward to what lies ahead"; that's how we win the prize.

Express It

As you pray, describe to God the "one thing" (v. 13) that you do in your relationship with Him. Mull aloud about the places in your life where you need His help in "forgetting," "straining forward" and "pressing on." Think about the help He has already given you and base your confidence on His faithfulness.

Consider It

As you read Philippians 3:12–21, consider these questions:

1) How did Paul compare his spiritual life to a marathon run?

2) What illustrations would you use from your life to explain Paul's view of the past?

3) Put Paul's ultimate goal in your own words.

4) How did Paul describe the right kind of examples for the Philippians to imitate?

5) How does the term "citizenship" (v. 20) help you explain your relationship with Christ and your participation in this world's affairs?

6) What picture did Paul use to describe those who were trying to sever the connection between Christ and the believers in Philippi?

7) In what ways does your pattern of spiritual growth parallel the one Paul described in these verses?

Grown-up Prayer Life

Today there is a renewed call within the Body of Christ to be a praying people. No matter where or when these times of prayer take place, the Bible teaches us that we can't be a grown-up church or effective church without a commitment to prayer. How often do you participate in prayer with others?

Philippians 4:1–9

4 Therefore, my brothers, whom I love and long for, my joy and crown, stand firm thus in the Lord, my beloved.

Exhortation, Encouragement, and Prayer

²I entreat Euodia and I entreat Syntyche to agree in the Lord. ³Yes, I ask you also, true companion, help these women, who have labored side by side with me in the gospel together with Clement and the rest of my fellow workers, whose names are in the book of life.

⁴Rejoice in the Lord always; again I will say, Rejoice. ⁵Let your reasonableness be known to everyone. The Lord is at hand; ⁶do not be anxious about anything, but in everything by prayer and supplication with thanksgiving let your requests be made known to God. ⁷And the peace of God, which surpasses all understanding, will guard your hearts and your minds in Christ Jesus.

Key Verse

"Do not be anxious about anything, but in everything by prayer and supplication with thanksgiving let your requests be made known to God" (Phil. 4:6).

⁸Finally, brothers, whatever is true, whatever is honorable, whatever is just, whatever is pure, whatever is lovely, whatever is commendable, if there is any excellence, if there is anything worthy of praise, think about these things. ⁹What you have learned and received and heard and seen in me—practice these things, and the God of peace will be with you.

Go Deeper

"Prayer and supplication with thanksgiving" (Phil. 4:6)—the Greek phrase means to cry out continually, humbly and gratefully for our needs and the needs of other people. We can pray about anything. And we do best when we pray about everything!

Prayer describes the systematic presentation of praise, worship and petition to God. Supplication seems to take things a little deeper and more personal—getting serious with God about the help we and others need from Him. Prayer expresses gratitude and interest in what God has done or will do for you.

But supplication adds intensity to your prayers. In Matthew 7:7–11, Jesus is describing prayer when He talks about asking, seeking and knocking. In prayer, we start by asking. Then we seek by being attentive to how God answers. And if we can't see or don't see His answer, we come and knock. In Luke 18:1–7, Jesus commended the persistence of the widow in seeking an answer from the judge, using that as an encouragement for us "always to pray" and not give up. Supplication tells God we're not giving up depending on Him. Supplication means we're knocking on God's door.

(continued)

Go Deeper Continued . . .

Prayer and supplication often appear together in Scripture. They are used together in Ephesians 6:18, 1 Timothy 2:1, and 1 Timothy 5:5. When a church desires to move on to perfect maturity—to grow up—prayer and supplication will become part of the living rhythm of the church. All this should be done in an atmosphere of thanksgiving. *Thanksgiving* means remembering what God has done—it fuels the confidence of our prayer and supplication.

How important is prayer in your church? Are you more or less prayerful than your church? What does recognition of a problem require? When you recognize a problem or weakness, God may be urging you to become part of the solution. At the very least, you should be diligent in your prayers for the local church of which you are a part, and saturate everything with gratitude!

Our first question for this lesson is this: What does a grown-up church pray about? Well, the short answer to that is *everything!* Paul told the Philippians (and us) to pray about everything! Pray about personal purity. Pray about good health. Pray about good marital relationships. Pray about happy children and physical safety. Pray about a growing mind. Pray that God will protect you from the evil one. Pray for the salvation of your family. The list goes on and on until it covers everything!

How do you think Jesus feels when He sees you and me rarely use a privilege that He paid for with His own life? Not to talk to God, not to fellowship with Him in prayer, is a declaration of our *independence* from God. It's a declaration of *insensitivity* to our privilege. It's also a declaration of *indifference* toward sin.

Prayerlessness cuts the heart out of a church. It stunts growth. If the only prayer we ever hear in church is the pastoral prayer on Sunday morning, if prayer is not a primary ministry of the church, it's a pretty obvious clue that our church is not yet mature. Prayer is an integral part of a grown-up church.

Why should the church pray? First, prayer is the way we talk intimately with God. Prayer is our channel of communication with the

"We pray because God moves His hand when we pray."

One who loved us so much that He gave His Son to die for us. It's the way we can show Him we love Him. It's the way we can tell Him we love Him. How would you like to be God and know that Your sons and daughters never wanted to talk to you?

Second, prayer is the best way to knit together the hearts of believers. When we pray together with other Christians, a bond is formed. Paul asked, "Finally, brothers, pray for us, that the word of the Lord may speed ahead and be honored, as happened among you" (2 Thess. 3:1). He understood that prayer has a powerful unifying effect.

Third, prayer is the desire of God. When we pray, we do what the Bible tells us to do. Jesus told at least one parable to convince men always to pray and not to lose heart. (See Luke 18:1.) Paul included a personal request for prayer in almost every letter he wrote. It's God's desire for you and me to pray. Prayer is a command in His Word. Paul wrote, "I desire then that in every place the men should pray" (1 Tim. 2:8). Prayer is what God wants. And you and I want to do what God wants.

Fourth, we ought to pray because prayer is a wonderful way to worship God—especially when we pray alone. That's the best time for us to be down on our faces before God, opening our hearts before Him, being humble before Him and letting ourselves be transparent to God.

Fifth, we pray because prayer is a terrific way to coordinate our needs with God's provision. Paul wrote, "And so, from the day we heard, we have not ceased to pray for you, asking that you may be filled with the knowledge of his will in all spiritual wisdom and understanding" (Col. 1:9). He heard about their faith and immediately knew what else they would need. So, he prayed for them. That's why the church gets together and prays, to rejoice in what God has done and anticipate what He will do.

Sixth, prayer proves to the world that we not only believe God exists, but that He is interested in our lives every day. When we pray, we tell the world we believe there's a God who is listening, a God who is involved in our lives and a God who wants us to talk with Him.

Seventh, we pray because God moves His hand when we pray (Acts 12:5–12). The hand of God does not work apart from prayer. Instead, when we are prayerless, we tie God's hands. Prayer brings revival; prayerlessness leads to deadness. We need a prayer-sparked revival in the Church today. Paul loved this church in Philippi because he knew they would pray for him.

Express It

A grown-up prayer life is not a possession or a continual state. Prayer is a lifestyle that must be constantly cultivated. It gets better with practice and worse with neglect. Given all the reasons for prayer in this lesson, choose two or three and talk to God about them as you pray today.

Consider It

As you read Philippians 4:1–9, consider these questions:

1) What does it mean to rejoice?

_____

_____

_____

2) In what ways does Paul both confront and compliment Euodia and Syntyche?

_____

_____

_____

3) What qualities did Paul expect the Philippians to exhibit as they proclaimed Christ to the world?

_____

_____

_____

4) What does it mean to you that the Lord is "at hand" still today?

_____

_____

_____

5) Which of the things worth thinking about (v. 8) do you have the hardest time keeping in mind? Why?

_____

_____

_____

6) When have you recently experienced the presence of the God of peace?

_____

_____

_____

God and the Grown-up Church

Local churches often struggle with the tension between using resources locally and sending them to far places. How much of the budget goes to missions? If we can't pay the light bill, should we continue to provide resources to send the Light?

Philippians 4:10–20

God's Provision

¹⁰I rejoiced in the Lord greatly that now at length you have revived your concern for me. You were indeed concerned for me, but you had no opportunity. ¹¹Not that I am speaking of being in need, for I have learned in whatever situation I am to be content. ¹²I know how to be brought low, and I know how to abound. In any and every circumstance, I have learned the secret of facing plenty and hunger, abundance and need. ¹³I can do all things through him who strengthens me.

¹⁴Yet it was kind of you to share my trouble. ¹⁵And you Philippians yourselves know that in the beginning of the gospel, when I left Macedonia, no church entered into partnership with me in giving and receiving, except you only. ¹⁶Even in Thessalonica you sent me help for my needs once and again. ¹⁷Not that I seek the gift, but I seek the fruit that

Key Verse

"And my God will supply every need of yours according to his riches in glory in Christ Jesus" (Phil. 4:19).

increases to your credit. ¹⁸I have received full payment, and more. I am well supplied, having received from Epaphroditus the gifts you sent, a fragrant offering, a sacrifice acceptable and pleasing to God. ¹⁹And my God will supply every need of yours according to his riches in glory in Christ Jesus. ²⁰To our God and Father be glory forever and ever. Amen.

Go Deeper

How well do you know the missionaries your church supports? Consider making it a special project to establish a personal connection between them and you and your family. When they come for a visit, volunteer to host them in your home. Your children will gain priceless lessons from the lives of those who are on the front lines in missions! But so will you. Be alert to special needs they may have that you can have a part in meeting. When a missionary comes to your home, think of yourselves as Philippians and

your guest as Paul. Read through Acts 16 with your family and discuss how Lydia hosted Paul and his team. How does that picture affect the way you treat your mission guests, the questions you ask and the way you pray for their ministry? Rubbing elbows with missionaries can help everyone in your family grow up spiritually just a little—and sometimes a lot. Many of today's missionaries trace their own call to missions back to visits from God's servants in their childhood homes.

A grown-up church gives and receives. A grown-up church learns that what it can give of greatest value is love. Love will never be diminished by giving but will actually grow as a result of being given away. Love expands as it is given. This understanding flows from a principle that we forget if we begin to think that genuine giving comes from *our* resources.

Paul devoted most of this section to acknowledging and appreciating the practical help he had received from the Philippians over the years. Epaphroditus had recently delivered "gifts" (v. 18), but the assistance from the Philippian church had begun almost immediately after the church was planted during Paul's first mission trip into Macedonia.

Paul began, "I rejoiced in the Lord greatly that now at length you have revived your concern for me. You were indeed concerned for me, but you had no opportunity" (v. 10). Paul didn't want to be misunderstood. He knew that the interruption in support by the Philippians had not been caused by their lack of interest but because of circumstances which had not given them "opportunity." Perhaps they lost track of Paul's whereabouts or they were told that the "famous" apostle no longer needed their help. Paul's gratitude is clear—"When you found out I had a need, you immediately took action to meet it." The Philippians' giving was personal. They sent Epaphroditus with gifts. The fact that Epaphroditus stayed indicates that the church commissioned him to remain at least for a while and help Paul. We can also assume that the "gifts" were more than just funds. It may not have included chocolate chip cookies, but the Philippian care package deeply touched the imprisoned apostle.

Even Paul's thank you notes include spiritual insight. He understood that giving and gratitude take on a deeper dimension when both the giver and receiver realize they are part of God's way of supplying needs. And make no mistake about it, God is divinely clever and creative in the ways He supplies *through* one part of His Creation to meet the needs in another part. That's the way He has always worked.

"God is divinely clever and creative in the ways He supplies through one part of His Creation to meet the needs in another part."

Here are a few examples of God's supply work:

- In Exodus 16, God provided for the people of Israel both manna and quails. Nature cooperated directly with God's purposes. The people didn't humbly petition God for help. They didn't even ask nicely. They complained. Yet God was gracious.

- In Ezra 1, God fulfilled a prophecy of Jeremiah's by instigating an order from King Cyrus of Persia that the temple in Jerusalem was to be rebuilt. God even made sure those who returned to Jerusalem would be taken care of through gifts of "silver . . . gold, with goods, with beasts, and with costly wares" (Ezra 1:6).

- In Nehemiah 1–2, a Jewish cupbearer in Artaxerses's court prayed humbly for God to intervene, and God provided a way and the means to rebuild Jerusalem through another powerful pagan king.

In Exodus, God met Israel's needs through nature. In Nehemiah, God gave to Nehemiah what he asked the king for. And Ezra shows us God can take care of things on His own if He wants to do that. God supplies differently in different parts of Scripture. How are we going to know where God wants us to put our money?

Let me suggest several giving principles from God's Word:

- First, the key element to funding the work of the Lord is the purity and integrity of those who are going to spend the money. The need may be real, but those promising to meet it may not have demonstrated integrity.

- Second, a grown-up church fosters a spirit in which giving aims for the right fit between the donor and the ministry. People need the freedom to give as God directs.

- Third, give out of the right attitude (2 Cor. 9:7). God may have given you the gift of giving (Rom. 12:8). If you have the right heart, it won't be hard for you to give in the grown-up church.

- Fourth, practice putting God first—literally. When it comes to giving, God doesn't get whatever we have left over. He gets it off the top.

- Fifth, we must recognize that we really aren't just giving—we're investing in what lasts forever.

There are numerous ways in which grown-up Christians and grown-up churches think and reach out beyond themselves, but the primary channel involves giving. God will supply every need, not simply so that we can feel "supplied," but so that we can participate in supplying others!

Express It

Before you pray, take a few moments to review your present giving patterns. Are you in "tithing autopilot," or do you consider needs and opportunities God may present every time you get a paycheck? Spend some time talking to God about your financial priorities, asking Him to direct the giving decisions you make.

Consider It

As you read Philippians 4:10–20, consider these questions:

1) What specific reason for rejoicing did Paul give in this passage?

_____

_____

_____

2) How did Paul explain the "secret" of facing life's ups and downs?

_____

_____

_____

3) What past events did Paul use to compliment the Philippians through their shared history?

_____

_____

_____

4) How did Paul understand the various benefits of giving? (See v. 17.)

_____

_____

_____

5) What comments did Paul make about the gifts Epaphroditus brought?

_____

_____

_____

6) In what ways is giving a component of the way you live your Christian life?

_____

_____

_____

7) How do you understand the connection between giving and growing up?

_____

_____

_____

The Cycle of Growth

Paul had high hopes for the Philippian church. They had proven themselves faithful and caring. The church had grown a lot but still had a lot of room to grow. Paul was eager to encourage them. He knew that spiritual growth should never cease this side of eternity. We can learn a lot from Paul and his relationship with the Philippians.

Philippians 1:1–2; 4:21–23

Greeting

1 Paul and Timothy, servants of Christ Jesus,
To all the saints in Christ Jesus who are at Philippi, with the overseers and deacons:
²Grace to you and peace from God our Father and the Lord Jesus Christ.

Final Greetings

4 ²¹Greet every saint in Christ Jesus. The brothers who are with me greet you. ²²All the saints greet you, especially those of Caesar's household.

²³The grace of the Lord Jesus Christ be with your spirit.

Key Verse

"The grace of the Lord Jesus Christ be with your spirit" (Phil. 4:23).

Go Deeper

Philippians 4:4–9 contains one of the most concise and powerful descriptions of mental health, soul health and heart health ever written. The verses are sometimes read as if they were a tribute to optimism, but their intent is almost directly opposite from "put on a happy face." Every one of these six verses provides a source for joy and peace outside ourselves. We don't invent joy; we let it infiltrate every corner of our lives. When we rejoice, we are reflecting, not creating, joy.

- First, we rejoice in the Lord (v. 4). Jesus is the source and target of joy.

- Second, joyful living flows out of the intimate awareness that "the Lord is at hand" (v. 5). The last words Jesus uttered before His ascension were,

"And behold, I am with you always, to the end of the age" (Matt. 28:20). When we behold the Lord's nearness, we rejoice.

- Third, joy flows when all our anxieties, needs and concerns are "made known to God" with thanksgiving (Phil. 4:6).

- Fourth, we find peace from God in Christ Jesus (v. 7), resulting in joy.

- Fifth, the subject matter of our thinking (v. 8) must reflect God's character and be worthy of joyful praise.

- Sixth, when we practice what God tells us (v. 9), joy as well as peace are constant by-products!

Philippians is a packed personal memo from the apostle Paul to a church he had founded. His message was both profound and practical. He shared both his vision for them as a grown-up church and his awareness of their shortcomings and challenges on the way to maturity.

There are several ways we can summarize the message of Philippians. Chapter 1 tells us that Christ must be central in our lives. Chapter 2 tells us why Christ is central and how important it is for us to be committed to Christlikeness. Chapter 3 reminds us that our ongoing responsibility to Christ involves not only growing in our knowledge about Him but also growing in our intimate, personal relationship with Him. And chapter 4 points out the purity that must characterize those who are claiming to live for Christ.

Major themes throughout Philippians highlight the characteristics of the grown-up Christian life. Paul mentioned joy or rejoicing in every chapter of this letter (1:4, 18, 25; 2:2, 17–18; 3:1; 4:1, 4, 10). Paul preached and practiced joy. No wonder this book has often been described as the great tribute to joy in the New Testament. (See Go Deeper.)

God's intimate involvement in our spiritual development is also covered in every chapter (1:6, 9–11, 21–29; 2:12–13; 3:12–21; 4:4–13). God began a good work in us and "will bring it to completion at the day of Jesus Christ" (1:6). God works in us, "both to will and to work for his good pleasure" (2:13). And no matter how far we get in the growing-up process in this life, the Lord Jesus "will transform our lowly body to be like his glorious body" (3:21) in heaven. As we learn to rejoice throughout life, "the peace of God, which surpasses all understanding, will guard your hearts and your minds in Christ Jesus" (4:7). We've got God's constant help on the way to growing up!

Unity is another central theme of Philippians and certainly a key component that ties many traits together in a grown-up church (1:27; 2:2–5; 3:3, 16–17; 4:2–3). Paul understood that unless the Philippians resisted the temptation to develop a religious "confidence in the flesh," their effectiveness to "shine as lights in the world" (2:15) would be seriously dimmed. The faith of the Philippians and every result that would follow needed to be seen in connection

> *"As we learn to rejoice throughout life, 'the peace of God, which surpasses all understanding, will guard your hearts and your minds in Christ Jesus' (4:7)."*

with Christ. Paul longed for them to grow up into the same vibrant relationship with Jesus expressed in the phrase "For to me to live is Christ, and to die is gain" (1:21). And he wanted them to develop that outlook *together.* So, one of his summary statements was, "Only let your manner of life be worthy of the gospel of Christ, so that whether I come and see you or am absent, I may hear of you that you are standing firm in one spirit, with one mind striving side by side for the faith of the gospel" (1:27).

As long as the Philippians were united in Christ, other examples of unity would naturally flow. For instance, as they experienced more and more of Christ's love, they would develop "the same mind, having the same love, being in full accord and of one mind" (2:2). These discoveries always take us back to Jesus' own words, "By this all people will know that you are my disciples, if you have love for one another" (John 13:35).

As if to underscore the centrality of Jesus, Paul began and closed his letter with words about Christ. Timothy and his servanthood (Phil. 1:1), the Philippians' sainthood (1:1) and grace (1:2) had their common source in Christ. The letter that followed was intended to renew the Philippians' realization that joy and everything else in the Christian life revolves around the Lord Jesus Christ. It's never about us—it's always about Him. So, it is no surprise that Paul returns to thoughts about sainthood in Christ and the grace of Christ in his final words. The apostle gave his Philippian brothers and sisters a glimpse of the wider reality of oneness in Jesus that extended all the way to "Caesar's household" (4:22).

Everything Paul packed into this memo and all the spiritual privileges that he rejoiced over, and longed to see every saint rejoice over, can be found only in "the grace of the Lord Jesus Christ" (4:23). All that we are and all that we have gets its meaning and is real in Christ. God's riches are not deserved, discovered or earned by us. We receive the assurance of all this even before we "have it," so, with Paul, we "press on toward the goal for the prize of the upward call of God in Christ Jesus" (3:14). And we keep referring to Paul's memo to the Philippians and the rest of God's Word for instruction and encouragement as we press on along the way.

Express It

Sit quietly before God and meditate on His grace. How do you know that God showers His grace on your life? In what ways has Jesus Christ demonstrated God's grace to you? Speak to God about the ways you see His grace in the world and about how that makes you want to respond.

Consider It

As you read Philippians 1:1–2; 4:21–23, consider these questions:

1) How do you explain God's grace demonstrated in Christ?

_____

_____

_____

2) What does it mean to you to be a saint?

_____

_____

_____

3) Why do you think Paul re-introduced himself to the Philippians in the opening of this letter as a servant, which also means "slave" or "bondservant"?

_____

_____

_____

4) When Paul wrote the final verse, "The grace of the Lord Jesus Christ be with your spirit," what results might he have been expecting, particularly in light of the letter?

_____

_____

_____

5) How central in your life is joy in Christ? In what ways?

_____

_____

_____

6) What thought or spiritual principle stands out the most for you in Philippians?

_____

_____

_____

7) What verses in this letter would you say most Christians ought to memorize and practice every day?

_____

_____

_____

Notes

Notes

Notes

Notes

Notes

Notes

Notes

Notes

Notes

Notes

Notes